# Illustrated Games of Patience

**Ben Estes**

The Song Cave

Published by The Song Cave
www.the-song-cave.com

Design and layout by Mary Austin Speaker



ISBN: 978-0-9884643-7-7
Library of Congress Control Number: 2014914208

FIRST EDITION

## Table of Contents

## Your Eager Neighbor

Open living and thinking
extracted from humiliation and shame,
the flower inside of the flower
should now be pretty easy to see
when the sea-tide shifts
and flocks of dogs graze
upon the salt marsh and treeless grasslands,
grazing for an herbal pastoral
they said couldn't be made.
It couldn't.
In the low cornfield of used cobbles and pebbles
the husky six footer eerily playing the didjeridu
turned his attention to the horseless carriage
so quiet and round it was hard
to tell if it was coming or going
up the steep crawl to the crest
to find if sincerity could indeed flower
in the hearts of this here tired ol' town.

I could not bear to see them as they had been,
the films of you teaching the movements of modern humans.
Enlarged to keep the dust from the hole,
most won't even see the motion. They'll just feel
the singing of advice from some saving-stamp scheme,
baiting them with a few cabbage leaves, tiny dribbles

wetting the rocks around the art deco shell mosaic.
A sadness our parents just didn't have time for.
How much longer can I hand you this line?

What is real...does it hurt?
Isn't it awfully late in the day
to be seeing purple hairstreak
pitting the sand?
Must it always be the tongue
glittering with quartz
in a welter of flying spray?

Anyway, a string of top jobs followed,
and I'll do my best to hold them,
as they do still show signs of decoration
for the nervous, excited, and I don't know,
maybe also the lost.
Four suns appeared in the African sky.
Sprung independently,
rolling off the assembly line,
a jigsaw puzzle
knitting peace
as common as bluebells,
then going back on into the earth at odd angles.
Times sure have changed since
we had to rear our babes in the dark
after hauling them out to breed.

## Board

Viewed from the side at sunset, my poem placed on the turtle grass in September referred to the others by their tens and elevens.

We walk to lakes in order to see our serenity reflected in them, and virtue and glory if it has not been settled – but it has, and a little of the warble of the martin, there.

Disturbed three different broods of partridges in my walk this afternoon.

When the earth has absorbed most heat, melons ripen out steep paths beyond springs.

## Is Boo Boo Hiding in The Blank of Blank

What will spring bestow?
A paper mask tied about my nose
looking like the whiskers of a cat,
or possibly more apt, a mouse.
Around you I am milkair,
or possibly more apt, tenderbluefog.
An everything evening I'm still unaccustomed to,
with the features of a blind parrot
flying through it over my town.
Knowing the place below is home,
but only able to let the few words I recognize,
a *Pretty Bird* or *Come Here*,
lead me to my branch.
Signaling the skill in this situation
is my lack of being able to describe it
within those two phrases.
The not-knowing cheers up
the knowing after all-
a shy quiet mouse that I tell to:
Pour water into saucepan.
Uncover bird.
Get bird water.
Get cigarette.
Put in mouth.
All are marks made without looking.

As even the best of us tire of these heroics,
we rest our eyes upon the dun colored fields
pictured in the evening doodles of hunters.
Also doodled:
Bugs, leaves, feathers, cracks in the ice, and berries.
In the feathers of parrots, dividing the sun with a paper mask,
a small dun field mouse.
In the juice of berries, a feather.

## African Violet Society

Hearing it go once, twice, three times a night...there was never a way our love could have seemed like a local disbelief, like antique ignorance. The two hands relaxing between us convinced us in their mistake, that we might have forgotten some nuance needed to preserve the spring flowers flooding the low fields along the bank, its depths as placid and nonchalant as the sea. We went out. We blew black smoke right on the old woman. We watched a bronze mask lit up by fire. We ate all the grasses in our field: violet then orange, pine, then the color of the desert sand blowing from across the low fields quicker than ever before. You could see how there couldn't be allowance, even then, for that loving hazel sky and rudeness of the lane.

No allowance to survive on, to pay my rent. These garden spiders demand I try to survive, earn a living, stay home most nights, and try to get my little talent together to write a poem for them every now and then.

## And There On That TV

In the humid orange moon
there was one, as if something
like breeze from a fan had stiffened it, and I,
cold and strategic, if I were to be,
I mean if all humans decided to be
wholly and truly, I refer
I refer to that human base rejection toward
they who have fled, burned and drowsy
by sunrise, we have
I have called it toward and found it musty and smelling
of cedar and hickory, held cupped
inside of another's other poem that I fumble with and pet
and carry home to push into deeper.
It's not the most difficult thing I have done
but it's close, exhausted and drugged for my frank work,
an elastic and spongy commonness
unpacked with whisky and music
making our right shoulders, then our left,
rolling onto and over then
our feet shoot out to the right and swing behind us,
we bend back at the waist in simple action,
then fall forward and all hands raised
into the strobe and orange
and blue and red with a half formed 4 behind us
flashed with drops of silver, trembling, shimmering and fair.

See, bodies do not pass all at once
but follow a series of
small awkward breaks
and often are brought back
hours later Juan says,
with my warm hug, Juan says
to play the role of night
with something more serious.
We sons of hunger haven't lost anything.
We don't know anything, have nothing left to sell,
we will try to help, will not betray
the distant desperate future of the world.
But the world isn't blessed to them
though they look at it with humble joy,
a winding and formless city
receiving these new lives, so there.

And also there on the TV is Duchamp
in the humid orange moon,
naively for the first time, no,
it was the second time,
saying woe unto him who unknowingly
is being filled with vital kind,
who threw himself over to the cause of defense.
Woe unto him who resists being filled
with the belief that the reason's reason
should answer our heart's heart.
Marcel goes on,

woe unto him who believes through stubbornness
rather than innocence that this at its spinning eternal beginning
will stand still and wait 3 years to say so, waiting,
like a humid orange moon to circle roughly and pull,
leaving a swollen reminder for tomorrow.
These steps thick through the snow,
a primitive instrument's pure music.

I'll push in as deep as I will now,
getting to the point of night now,
the one you most want to know. "It isn't only
about its value," Lazarus says, his hard-on heavy
upon waking, silhouetted against the rising sun.
My eyes fall downward,
and harden as dew does,
in the dark beneath the rough
shudders, and is of the flat ground
as your face opens up
affectionately so to pour,
or purr, and adjust the power and volume of the sound.
Conquer these bodies I have mouthed,
there is no one alone
here in a way I can approach or form but a
warmth and turning of face,
a tender delicate
lovely generous face, lovely and abundant,
touching and chinning against the jaw through honest aspects
lovely and lapping.

We'd dreamt of this drawing of the face
breaking the surface of the stream.

We'd also hoped to suit shadow and turn the stage
into an eager aquarium – for Admiration
to sing there in between us: "Away
with superstition, loneliness, and generation!
His body and the dreamed-of release
turned the wine stained rag
back into grape and snapping grace,
crossed with a new violence
of louder and intenser music.
Please, think twice before crossing
over my winter lake
from cape to cape, from glance to glance,
forced and feeling fatigued -
to go to see him only
to send him back on his way,
to follow his visions,
his breaths,
his body and his day."

Driving up in the borrowed car
with no tune to play
or map, for the drive
to see the gray capped
pink socked babe carry me back
to lay a new ash boundary around the foot of the fireplace.

We, whistling down the blue-green rainbow
seen pasted to the stormy sky outside,
admit to one another our times
confusing the wild beast with tame parrot.
The days when we could ask
to replace
one word with another
word too hot or too tragic.

If to be forgotten
by a kind of fear,
and lonely awkward tallness,
or a sweet glance sensitive and phallic
mixing the whole plastic bag of bits
to find the exact match to the gem missing
from the hilt of your casually simple steps,
a thrown coat on the floor of the bar,
sleepy and watching TV, my split open pine.
Time and tired and relax and lay and read
the lyrics printed on the inside of the gate-fold,
between the licking and smoking
reciting them then through the electric fan
with the careful tracks of voice tuned to these unsimple sets.

So then I feel the need to thank it,
your crooked piece of man,
and speak to it
as if it were a microphone

to amplify and replace
the absent tiredness of these lines.
Knowing that experience does not equal knowledge,
and not by this confusion of involving and inloving means
one single blooming bird of paradise
set inside of a hippy ceramic mug,
placed by sure hands atop a postal flat-rate box
in front of a Mexican tapestry.
He'll be born, live, and await his reincarnation
in the bronze décor, or is it gold -
that little dot of gold to place both our hopes upon,
to hold my head, to hold my arms,
and carry me back -
a black silhouette behind
a towering black field.

Draw on and draw forth dear
citizens, to observe this fearless play
where one can assume the sympathies of the kneeler
on the opposite side of this dry grey wall.
I cry in the morning.
Yes, and all winter, too. Crying,
and re-reading the apology
of here, to here.

## Clearest Call

Do ghosts ever take a single shape
to shape the way we decide to beg
for rain to run the chimney down
and wash the glare from roof-slates blown
between textured fair weather dew, and peace?

## A Rainbow Sign

I just don't think that
this is what it's supposed to feel like,
shaking my big one to break the stream
and make a pool for moving my tools,
for they weigh only half as much
when moved under water.
I emerged in the morning, covered in blood and fine acid sand
and decided to remain partially submerged a little while longer.
Itching for more exercise,
and cooled not by water but by air,
I spent the afternoon collecting sea shells,
and found each one heavily carved
with the numbers of pretty village girls
offering to take tourists to the ultimate level.
A spring and summer service they offer.
I meant to call one, with a headline ready on my lips,
but a gull would dive down wheeling and screaming
each time I tried to dial.
One can fool the animals,
but must forgive this wild, beautiful country.

## The Selected Texts of 12:34

The one hundred layers
of this onion and
the one hundred figures
made with this string can
explain how rock
can grow over rose
and how the games
of patience can teach us
to find an alright way
to feel a little lonesome
breathing in other's snores
and familiar crotches
in another's home zone
while taking pictures
sent for me to see
while I make soup for friends
labeled "QT" or an eye-roll
without having to say
much of anything
although selfishly not caring
being back home here and
how bored you'd be
of me for the night
is with you now in LA
without having much of anything

to even be able to imagine
after California'd brought you so much
fertile yarn to tie off of
winter to leave me nurturing
our calcified flowers
and choosing to not ask
while others keep on
asking and responding I'm not sure
being neither farmer nor botanist
while this still-point of Estes Gate
has parts as moldy as an old rock
though still fawn with downy skin
inside my pocket
around the fruit
the curious ivy curls
having no idea why
to not let it keep climbing
as it's not quite capable
of rotting out completely
and I guess it can still remind
of the paused summer that fed it
where all breaths were deep
and tails held erect while splashing
around in the welcome news

## A Pagan Décor

Hazel Sky was what we named the kitten
we'd found taking its first hesitant steps,
reminding us of the full nets of a fishing boat
and the simple distance between two people
allowing them to be able
to live with one another –
trying to remember that distance
set between the silent audience
and the performer's elitist position
of us vs. them
trying to remember the film set
with all those piles of leaves
burning in the background –
there was the beginning
the middle, the end, the dialog…

## The Fielding

Dinosaur footprints across those flat mud rocks along the river —let's plan a picnic there this summer, and spray them gold to use as foundations to build our thoughts of the end of this world, as they casually appear from the clock across the hall.

No one's yet disappeared. We went to the basement as told, and took a laptop with us to listen to Vintage Violence and nap, then back upstairs to find blue papers stacked outside the bedroom door, sprayed gold with white-paper cologne.

The cat died in the night, so we didn't have a place as ours as the glare of skylight obscured the grain our fingers were to have read in the raised wood. What for. What for what for what for. Oh, how we well. Oh, how we well up swell and span. Oh, how we span. Oh, how we spire, and highlight the bumps and cracks in between the boards all the way on into the kitchen, wanting to lie down there, as the ceiling gets darker and wetter and starts to drip the bulge to where they were lying down with mummy, and now fully aware of the end, and of the world, and not wanting to ask for any more info.

## Wishing Out Loud For The Pipe's Uphill End

As if looking at orange flowers
long enough would turn them blue, friend

## A Chimney Pot

All the work put into the chimney pot boiled down to a smoky turd, sun-dried and scattered over the worms in the ash.

This smell of myrrh incense, after a crotch swipe and sniff of my finger, is our waited-for dawn signal.

The lambskin. The crocodile skin. The shiny calfskin piping. The muslin. The nature of patchwork uniforms now marching around the garden in handsome overall vegetable cloche.

Halfblue trousers felled thickly opal next to the piper on the sand.

## Strength-Through-Joy

They came in droves to find inspiration
on the terraces of these beautiful old buildings
now just housing gift and craft shops.
And although we had been warned,
we were still horrified to see the women
squat, washing out their rags in the rapids
while the men in a similar action pan for gold.
Their faces done up in masks of comedy or tragedy
one half good, the other odd.
Not a story of mine, but a story for me,
of learning to benefit from the work of others.
Manhandled, perhaps to mid-chest,
thankful for the reminder that another
day has come and passed, just like the day before.

## We'll See How the Humans Have Changed It

The need to duck underneath the color of that sunset
was all that I wanted to give you.
Surprising to find out how easy it is when you have it right,
how I figured out what I wanted you to have
as the thin gels were put in
in front of the lamps.
I know that they weren't in the store when I was
there, instead you came home
with something small, wooden and chipped.
This is called *Blue Glass Dice and The Sandalwood Comb.*

It's tough to maintain that level,
when you want to touch me, to put
your hands on my shoulders, hold my hand,
me lying on the beach like a tool, or bowl, or both.
I don't know... what do *you* like to do?
Windows at night. You'd never know it
but I'm like you.
The things I trust, by nature, are endless
and can only be seen every few months
when the tide is out, like what
music is to blank tape, where I believe I used to live once
a long time ago, with a pear,
in a still life. This is called *The Guitar, and Other Machines.*

My specific tastes
in men really don't matter
now, I want to tell you
over and again that the last thing I want
is the endless cycle of liberty and regret
to be sent out to the rock pile for our gains,
my desire to get smarter people to talk about me
so that others can hear,
how they came down from Vermont with a stow-away fox
in the trunk of their car
and their tires got frozen to the curb.
Why doesn't anyone want to come back with me when
I can see from the top where the beach is?

Hard I've worked, but
others come along
more efficiently.
I'm too sweaty and tired to arrange to go
home with somebody tonight.
We've had so little help here these days
since everyone has quit, that even
important logs have rolled into
the fire
unnoticed,
and I was never going to have sex again,
and a distant relative came to take over
to nurse me back to health and help out with our weeding.

All humans waiting for the will to change,
yet still able to be recognized
through sunlight and dark.
And happy.
In a few days, it is everyone's
job to join the workers,
to be here when no one else is.
A clean uncovered window
is all anyone wants. Bless you.
There's no reason to be upset by this fighting.
Make sure the kids get considered,
and are sent back into the woods
once they have recovered a bit from the noise and grumble.
How should the others cope in the meantime?
Who's tending the garden?
I guess it isn't more important this season over any other,
this year we'll have to burn it off so they can host their dance, and
that the others who wish to join in are able to do so.
This is what all of our time is devoted to now,
who is running to the other,
who is reacting,
who is falling.
That may be an exaggeration, turning one's head to pride
in order to catch someone else's.
This is called *The Pebble That Turned Into a Pea.*

I lost, for how does one indeed carry this through?
Getting the intent. Becoming the trial
between thick and thinly lived living.
Not that I wasn't glad
to be able to offer my kind of assistance.
And not just for those to die far away
with weather dependent upon
the chorus returning from west to east,
or to pick the ripe ones before the squirrels
knock them from the trees to the ground.
Unfortunately it worked, we were both attracted.
And now that we have both succeeded
there is nothing left to do but
find even smaller pieces that become more handsome
the smaller they get.
I'll take responsibility for this poem
even though I didn't write it.

You can come back now.
Now that everything is starting
to be what it has to be, and
always has been, the summer is over.
The flashing flecks of mica in the
stone release it, but forget feeling it,
so as to be able to construct
a small song, our prayer,
to double our turns or conversions
into the middles of whatever separate rooms
we now find ourselves living.
To the mountain camps we've both come to
to be healed.
To be chosen by the hawk-faced chaperone
to dance with my new legs and
new sense of intent
between thick and thin living.
The intervals to which longing both led us,
at the end of the day, turned
out to be not so tragic after all: just ornate,
non-functional, and nocturnal.

The beach at night is endless.
With small fires floating useful at the horizon,
their columns add up and drop the ash of guilt
onto the forest at our back, not helping your
allergies, but adding
the necessary ph to the soil
for the berry bushes to grow.
Their roots hold the loose dirt of the hillside in place
to prevent mudslides, and
provide shelter for the mouse
to build its nest
and eat the larva
that destroyed so many
of our trees this time last year, remember?
And what if analysis and desire finally sided?
What if it was desire that finally led the two?
A lake in a volcano is what you see
and don't care to see any other way out of it.
It must be
because I have no
habitual way of making things, skills
lost and ignored, yet in appreciating
originality I feel quite at home,
looking at things from a different time

that do not belong to me,
this audience.
This is called *The Silver Tray, Reflecting A Flower.*

Yet, I keep try to sing these old
traditional songs
without any real words to sing,
hearing something aligned
beside these waves on the beach, my throat
unneeded, an electronic music
coming up from inside our hollow earth,
a bubble of tar and complicated prehistoric order
in whose haze your image trembles
and eludes me, and I say
*Good God, please.*

It's getting dark I'm afraid.
We should head home, but I
wanted to wait until you'd
answered the question.
Why it gains weight in our minds
every single summer,
lounging in shorts
among others in theirs,
never to be exposed. Tell me,
did I ever come to you
talking like this, in all these voices,
and you took me into you, me complaining how
miserable I'd been, staring up as a babe
from the comfort of his king's checkered horse?
This one is called *The Self-Portrait, and Other Ruins.*

Tonight, underground
with the smell of rocks, the air is fresh and clean
and we have seen signs of people up above,
and they were watching, as we do.

## Animal, Vegetable, Mineral

Tadpoles stretch in fountain beds
as red swans under red lights

cut a crystal mind upriver

Moving with a moving flame
a collector of Navajo rugs, agate and dog carvings

gifted to all who slumber sound

With the breath of a boogie in my hair
the night drive turns the bedroom handles

I rose and found shining dew on every buttercup

The friendly cow all red and white, I love her with all my heart
she gives me cream with all her might

to eat with apple tarts

Among the desert sands
some deserted city stands

urging cord to describe the fair curves

Orange in large black letters, or
Holy Ranch of supernatural terms

for growing two dirty tulips from China

Identified as dots and dashes
an enchanted throat consoling

under flickering candle light, an ice marble rolling

That state was filled with
pickpocket testimony from the hospital,

yes, and Peggy loves the country despite herself

Would you rather share him or extinguish him
begins the second part

now roomy from intimate contact with smaller tribes

Mineral a mineral of hunting
stunting the segment characters while

centurions offer sleeping peasants fowl

## With Napoleon and Josephine, the Woman of Paris, 1925

"It's like a bit of display, I think," searching about these mountains of France, standing with their loyal peaks and condemning our bouncy baby world huddled underneath the chestnut tree.

To my right, on a small tea table, is propped a portrait of the King of Rome, sitting on top of a sheep. To his right, two gold cups from Napoleon's toilet set.

The moon droops under the heat waves above the fire, as do the silhouettes of 3 parakeets sleeping in the warm updraft above it, lined upon a single branch.

"Dance with the globe and dream of this, this last civilization. These dreams of the *end of the world*!"

"Suffer this vision: the ecstatic esthetic possibility of pushing it all the way through the one you love!"

In being willing to say that in being willing to love one must be willing to lose. To give it all away and do as greyhounds do with Napoleon and Josephine, the Woman of Paris, 1925.

## Board

Are not the more tender the most downy?

The impurities of which color the foam and can be arranged in such pleasing forms, etc. along the walls and fences.

But the real beauty of the house, he told us, was to drive around to the lake behind it, where you can see the results of their old business, etc. It's really not surprising how that works.

A background of positive peppery flavor, and the water just yellow and green with a tang all grouped behind it.

Red-eye, Tanager, Pee-wee, etc. The leaves dry ripe like the berries.

## Can I Get There By Candlelight? Yes, And Back Again

By morning I will have forgotten
the plink of the banjo-clock,
rabbit-nibbled and trying to make
itself invisible in the mid-afternoon sunlight.
Remember that day
we tooketh the bronze ray
of shyness straight between the eyes,
and shared an egg?
Night fell, the nightjars churred
and laughed at our plaster guitar
Ula lu, la la lu lu

We'd searched all night, both
in front and behind the cameras,
and when we found it
grown by eye through trade and by blood,
there was still plenty left over
to buy some other flowers
for the pretty woman
dressed in male clothing
treating you, my reader,
like the intelligent friend you are.

## A Bloom in Glory

Our casual interpretation
of decency is noted
by the thick cadaver flower
that soandso breeds, looking
like a lavender hog
with a belly full of thrift, soft mud and rice.
The fetid flower still survives
as a grave god,
within shouting distance of that place
where that movie was filmed in the river
now paused by the beam of our flashlight. Literally
at the end of the earth, as the earth itself uttered it.
Ula lu, la la lu lu.

## From *In The Ceiling* to *A Seaside Town*

In the ceiling, in the basement, as insulation and social secrets.
Saw the frog's head sticking out of the ground. Turned it up.

Stuffed with excelsior. Then, to put a line border on the rim.
Motorcycles to split the crowd.

Sulfur, and phosphorus in the eyes of a horse.
Just as good as finding money, maybe even better.

A beautiful ten minute dig. Earthy cider and blue kernels.
Smoke in still air, without any formal seed.

A marigold in a pink sparkle of light.
Adam's apple, bobbing in the window of a seaside town.

## Will Lunch Be Offered As An Optional Extra?

Tired of walking and checking the lines
of the tourist train that trundles through
this town, famous for its pottery
and brackish dune pools once visited
by St. George and his dragon, and the lady with her unicorn,
I stopped at a convenient place to sit and shuck my sweet corn
and let the local men hang their gates from my eyes.
All they could offer were other versions of myself:
soft and sweaty, sick of the big car diet dished up by Detroit
and the cocktail-party and locker-room chatter
I've had to tackle while touring this country's musky beaches.

Choosing to drive to my next stop, I found
perched upon a tall chalk cliff
the statue of a broad-bodied chaser
so large I could never easily handle him as a top.
He'd been added on to so many times over the centuries,
that it was only really possible to identify him by touch:
a little more shy, perhaps, than other guys his age,
an abstract clock-face jutting from the pack
I could feel buckled around his waist,
and such wee-wee nuts,
he could only be named, I whispered, *Patience.*
I camped there in his shadow 'til noon the next day,
and drove away leaving a few of my burnt bones there, behind.

## Stockholm Minus Utrecht Equals Half

The deep grooves we've made,
that everyone has by now heard about,
harden as the fields fade out and get noisy
and as the pudgy children that we've avoided
from connecting to this flat seascape somehow
have gone and planted pretty Parrot Tulip
bulbs on down the side of our drive.

Tenderness, being the exact same thing. It's like that too.
It'll stand still and shrink in different ways
than misfortune ever could,
with the expansion and swelling
easily seen. The deep beat felt
inside of any bad luck – as it does
in many other things, gloom can't.

There is food packed
inside this sweet, warm, black, lucky garden.
Lucky, since sarcasm has yet to make us many friends.
We had no idea that'd be the case –
indeed we found these fields
fertile, fool, yet as soon as we tried to cover it up
it went all pebbled, pock-marked, and shrunk.

Eventually, every morning
will dispel the idea that I am just like them.
I'll say "next year" next year
if the summer winds up there are weaker –
but summer suns are just so turquoise
green and the night rise so far beyond any revolving bloom.

We'd gone ahead and hardened into our related arrangements
so that we could leave them wondering
if they were that similar before we'd found them –
and the sky was darkening far out over the thick ice,
held cradled in your arm,
surprised somewhat, I know,
but then I could see me, as I would look to myself
hiding from someone rudely,
and the look that came along with that
was enough.

Now instead, all of the ranges around you have started to flatten,
and if you've smoothed and fancied
your guilt too little, at the end of the day then
what stance can really be ours?

*

Back in the city nothing was dim
or spontaneous, like the green striped sailboats
pulled around the pond by little boys with strings,

circling on around back to our side.
Our side, revealing a lot more of what we thought
than our wooden skeletons ever could.
You'd realized that. Therefore then
our customs will always appear only customary
to the misers diligently picking the lane free
of catalogues or bottles and cans.

It was all so difficult, without knowing anything
of the well-lit bricks ever appearing
to be even or a sand-filled odd. Instead,
just my stupid and naïve idea of the whole,
as lovers in a stereo view,
stumbling around with the tin cans
out in the junk field before leaving
to sit here next to you, warning them
strongly and paying no attention
to what was best or least likely.

What is actually surprising I guess,
is that one needs to make a big deal of it at all
as if it weren't actually a part of truly living.
But then that idea too idles and turns
into something that sinks down to the bottom,
beeping from the deep that it wants to be nearer,
convincing, but pointless in pinning down
the jingle now lost for a while in the mud.

*

Behind me, short benches sit along the water
and a small speaking part.
I refused it so to work around it and relax into being ignored.
Snap judgments and idleness I guess were required,
although no one's ever suffered much by being visited
by the ghosts of the past, present or future.
Stupid strands do weave through though,
despite my conservative efforts,
and decorate rather than reveal
another isolating look towards care.

As the tadpoles stretch out in the fountain beds,
letters eventually get written after misting
the pile, then letting them again dry up.
Sometime in the next few years
I'm hoping it becomes worthwhile,
though it'll never actually ever
be soon enough, the dreary differences
vanish, as it doesn't matter to the weaknesses
of this climate's missing rise.

## The Light of This Half

The light from this half-flame's clown made,
and rarely able to fully engage
with the sloppy top layer, let alone
the one at the end
as shade looms spread open the cloth
to mark our birth
as we and our kind are forgotten,
frightened, walking over the bridge and unable to talk
or even turn our head
to the sweet planted offer that'd been laid to distract me,
but want to put mine aside
and hopefully make myself
for yours.

## Undoubtedly

The man flying from the thing he dreads
mistaken by the man who seeks the thing he loves,
unconcerned by the time of day,
joyed without dazed eyes,
chose happiness
without rash decisions or any bad language –
as if the desert's maturing
were purely a social pleasure set aside
by all sweet sounds and harmonies.

A special right to laugh then,
and a large part of the body breathes and sees things in life,
like the sun glancing off the orange temple casting cast-offs,
or these terrifying elements creating fossils
of summer corals and shellfish
indicating that soft hums of isolation
among secluded scenes and deeper tanks
support clear skies, and vent these pastoral farms.

These little unremembered acts of kindnesses and loves
give gifts and return to you. They all turn to you
with village harvests moistening clouds above.

## From *A Painter of Snails*

If the card isn't getting home fresh
Then it's never getting home at all.
If the home isn't ever a fresh card,
Then there never was a home.
If there never was a card,
Then the transparent eyeballs
Were never really invisible,
Just card eyeballs.
If the card eyeballs were to step
Out to where my heart is,
Then my heart would get home freshly.
If my heart got home freshly,
It would surely scare
My little black pup to obey.
My puppy, home
Waiting patiently with baited eyeballs, paws
On invisible, transparent cards, kissing and stroking this fresh heart o' mine
to lone pine to
spit shine
to judge's fine to
white wine
to fishing line to
serpentine
to pumpkin vine to

dollar sign
to ball of twine to
reassign
to soaked in brine to
number nine
to opaline an opaline to

Easily Discouraged
read this slowly,
Drop Greek rhythm and
Drop roll's videoed-
For mine eye'd
Glory hole be
Nothing without this
Dirty round shadow video

## No title yet

Consider the form of an artifact,
the material in which it's made –
A right eye, a left eye,
after right eye, after left.
One needs to make those decisions.
Paint eyes simply
to keep things living, and in
searching find the spectacles
while tapping trees
for the oil of the fragrant crotch
that melts as it's rubbed
into the wood and our new style –

If people could believe in anything
if anything could be possible –
You'd have had to have been there –

Set swallowed a bit of Horus'
semen (indirectly, on a lettuce leaf)
and gave birth through his forehead
to a golden disc, the moon
which, rising in Uranus at my birth,
accounts for my love of precision.

## Marbled Bells in the Bath Can't Block the Sounds From the Next Booth's Video

While working up lathers to hide
that ugly is only skin deep,
I feel small trout grow portly under water
to belly my upwind line
and distract myself by watching the ravens play
in the updrafts, like sexual summer migrants
taunting the doves that I'd brought in disguised as underwear.

Holding my breath, I listen
to the architectural echoes bouncing
off the dandy walls made of coral,
and decide to just lie down and rest for a while,
feeling less pleasurably punctuated than I thought I would,
as the lost arts seem to have been lost
to the other naked bodies in here
splaying out as near a definition of forever as exists.

## Board

How long will this beautiful purple be part of this deep cut? It seems more days these days end with a beautiful purple.

I grew one-third larger. It looked like a rose in water.

Olive green, with gold bands.

It's really not surprising that it works.

By working together we've now managed to exchange our lack of wheat for flowers, and for poppy, poppy now is.

## Cymbals

It's ok I will say    And it's alright    I stop    and wonder    if a triangle sounds    as the turning thurns    grabbing their ankles for flutes and for cymbals    Ankles, cymbals and flutes come and go    and came    and went

*Picture a painting of flowers, white flowers made out of something like marble carved to look like cloth. Nothing is as vulnerable as a flower, and this is a painting of a flower and a flower's container. Sometimes the containers of things seem unfinished, when they actually are finished. That that is the way it finishes. Sometimes it goes and goes, and sometimes it just looks like it.*

The question doesn't question    coming or going    or came or went    it's not about    being tried or tired    but of trying and tiring    not about a town inside of a town    but of a cymbal or flute    how cymbals and flutes tire    a flower inside of a town a tiring flute inside of a flute    I will say stop and it will    and I wonder    if the flute will sound like cymbal or belly    or hooky and flower    because it sincerely did flower    and go to tired town    It came back a flower    a cymbal    and a flute    Yes it did    and it did    and it did    And the flute    come and go come and go    come and go

*The varnish of flowers made the white man of flowers act something like variegated marble carved to reflect a flower. Nothing is thusly as*

*vulnerable as a flower and it's varnish. A flower container and a flower. Sometimes the tops of the containers seem open ended when in fact the containers are closed. That's the way that is right for a rabbit to compare. Sometimes it just goes and it goes and the taste is barely even noticeable.*

The sound of a cymbal is corrected    I will call it good    I will say that sentence and they    will establish the power    through a sometimes astonishing smile    Then I stop    and I wonder if a triangle    will in fact make a sound    like "to be" or "insignificant absence" or "school"

Oh you have made the spin    that seizes their spilling    for rabbits and for cymbals    spilling cymbals    or rabbits that are coming with company    You never come and go    and how much of the thought    that they have thought    compares and scares the rabbits    as they come    to the city inside the city of the cymbal    or the rabbit as the cymbal    that makes the rabbit tire out    a rabbit inside of a rabbit

I will say that sentence    and I will wonder    if the rabbit sings of cymbals    or of schools    or the insignificant absence    of schools and of flowers    or of blooming    and going to the city five seconds before arriving    Frankly make the flower    for he has gone on to tired town    and has returned a flower    a cymbal    and a rabbit    Yes he made it    and made it and made it    and the rabbit comes to compare    the sound's power    and smiles clearly at the time    that's reserved for the making

Then I stop  I have a triangle  that is saying "We will be"  or "now do it with effect"  "it is an insignificant absence"  and "go to school"  Voices never thought that way  but it was true what it said  that the youngster full  of the hope of open hearts must hear voices he believed  were from the time reserved for the making  That he was made at the same time  it was to go and is going  Saying it made it honest  and it made it  and it was honest  and it made it so  and it said it was

Oh we made it  arrived  and also made it so that  apprehending the spots  on the rabbit's fur was easier  to make the kitty-cornered spots kiss  and make up  Rabbits come with society Yet rabbits never come  and how ever many thought  that they had had the thought  is in comparison to the rabbits  and their fear  that they come  and that they were

I will say this phrase  and I will sing it to the rabbit  with kitty cornered spots on its fur  or to the schools  or to the insignificant absence  of the missing schools  and missing flowers  for they have blossomed  and the town will take five seconds to arrive  Become honest said the flower  become a tired town

And the flower growing on the edge  of the basin of consonance  says that the rabbit has come back  yes it made it  yes feel and feel it  The rabbit comes to compare  comes to compare  comes to compare

*Rabbit says the varnish of the flowers that made the white man of the flowers share something will be made from marble carved to reflect a flower. Rabbit turned and talked back, that's sure. As a woven man now. Your choice to believe in your type of belief. An argument to it in this way still swims as vulnerably as a flower and it's varnish. Like a container for a flower inside of a flower. The way that it finishes is a way that must be compared. Compare the rabbit to a taste that is barely, yet exactly, perceivable.*

It goes on   in the form of the fact   and of the sincerity that it
had   been made and it made   and then it made it vulnerable:
business needed to be finished   before it made the return   on
tired pins and needles   for the flutes and cymbals   pins
cymbals   flutes   come and you go   and thus far have only
thought only thus far for this

Not tired by the city inside of the city   or of flutes as cymbals
or the tiring of vulnerable flutes   because flowers are the way
they are   in spite of all of the flowers   that everyone arrives
carrying   into tired town   They carry tired flutes inside of
flutes   and they say "the orientation   and alarm of flutes   love
either stomach   or hooky and flower   or flutes inside of flutes
or pins and needles that go   to the city five seconds before arriving"

Then because the form of the fact   that sincerity flowers in
tired town   we gave back the flowers   and the flutes   yes we
made it   and made it   and made it   and hey   flutes come
and go   and go   and go

*Nothing is as vulnerable as an old flower, and this here is a picture of a container flowering, as it itself is a flower. Sometimes this is the true way to observe it. And sometimes the containers of things seem incomplete, that they need some real finishing. That this is the way that this one will end. That this is the accurate way it will go. Sometimes it goes, and it goes, and sometimes it is even accurate.*

## Board

The lice on the birches make it very disagreeable to go through them, unless you can join hands with a good worker and somehow produce more, together.

Such great shells must have made convenient household tools.

Even the hinder part of a mud turtle's shell is scalloped, one would say rather for beauty than for use.

He said that in the beginning, naked, a steep path would lead to the spring and welcome a relief of beauty, viewed from the side at sunset.

I saw partridge hatchlings too, and earth and glory yet resolved.

## No Title

That this mountainside looks like a face is accidental,
which is a shame, for I dearly love to laugh.
The touch-smoothed redwood cross-section, in its rings
of growth and brightness,
seems like a sun seen from underwater,
wobbly as jelly, mocking my
inability to find a job, my food stamps,
and saddens me to see
the teens tagging themselves in nearby places
to earn a virtual friend's respect, or boasting
other symptoms of youth while leaving
their greasy fingerprints on the thick lenses of my glasses,
mocking my desire for artwork
to remain packed in straw, and in music
for sleepers halfway awake to grow wild in.

It all gives me faith in arranging, I guess,
when there is nothing else I seem much good at but fuss
and copy and paste, with a head full of so many other worries.
Got a check today. Bought a book I can't read
without it putting me to sleep
with its out-of-date luxuriousness.

So instead of reading it,
I stayed up and listened to Harry Partch's song

*And on the Seventh Day Petals Fell in Petaluma,*
dedicating it to the memory of Ramon Novarro,
hoping it would arch electrically above him
with all the characteristics of fire
all night,
all day,
and soak his early spring colors in a late autumn
sun as pale as silver and fern-green skies

*to draw light*
*through midnight*

and steer instead his valley's vista
toward my own simple neighborhood loneliness
with nothing better to do than lie back and lecture
those cultured Internet boys
on their own death's primitive and permanent cartoons,
to walk carefully and not step on any snails,
the poor,
the rough skin bundles,
or shiny boners poking out from satin robes.
This light, is dark.
And on the seventh day petals fell on Petaluma,
forgiving those who hurried past before
stuffed with poo and feathers underneath the hot yellow heat
that I wish would ignite all the unopened envelopes
piling up on the table by my front door,
(and burn up all of the time I've spent

on all of the things I can't
put my finger toward).

I went for a walk this evening
and found a speckled turkey egg
where the river settled
into the mud of the salt flats.
I looked at the burnished iris
of the eye of a trout.
A gleaming Atlantic coin.
Thinking even the wind tonight could speak,
blowing in seeds not yet caught
on the coat of the dog. Still, life.
And all the needs in this world.

## Board

Walking to the lake to look at the mouth
because it is easy to find fire in the plant,
the purple, the color of the navy sky hook.

A little hook
of purple flame projecting from the field and into the air.

## Hearing Summer Horns

Turn on the lamp, close the blinds to the lone headlight of the bicycle riding through the dark to your window. Walk on out into the field at night once everyone is asleep, toward the tree line, and masturbate there in the dark. For the figures of open mouths in the shape of a B, then an E, then N, spelling "Boards" and "Summer Horns."

A children's book illustrator built this building, is still building this building, around the light pockets and jellyfish filament of the new bulbs. To the statues of dogs through the windows, and in return to the dark of the house.

So, to each his own. Let each have their own, and let's allow liberty to write her own name to a bronze mask and the notion of the false, lit by fire. For the need to live out an outpost, finding oneself as we do, and more when the sun goes.

## Acknowledgements

Thank you to the editors of the journals *BafterC*, *Fanzine*, and *Jubilat*, where a few of these poems first appeared.

Some of these poems also appeared in: *The Strings of Walnetto Arrangements* (Flowers & Cream, 2011); in the one-person exhibition *Loose Boards,* at Nepenthes NYC, 2012; and in Engineered Garments Fall/Winter 2012 lookbook. Eight of these poems were also translated into Japanese and published as the chapbook *8 Poems* (Engineered Garments, 2012.)

OTHER TITLES FROM THE SONG CAVE:

1. *A Dark Dreambox of Another Kind*, by **Alfred Starr Hamilton**
2. *My Enemies*, by **Jane Gregory**
3. *Rude Woods*, by **Nate Klug**
4. *Georges Braque and Others*, by **Trevor Winkfield**
5. *The Living Method*, by **Sara Nicholson**
6. *Splash State*, by **Todd Colby**
7. *Essay Stanzas*, by **Thomas Meyer**